Let's Talk About
BEING FORGETFUL

Let's Talk About
BEING FORGETFUL

By JOY BERRY

Illustrated by John Costanza

Edited by Kate Dickey

Designed by Abigail Johnston

GROLIER ENTERPRISES CORP.

Let's talk about BEING FORGETFUL.

Forgetting is not remembering.
When you forget something you do not
think about it. You do not remember it.

Have you ever forgotten to do something?

Have you ever forgotten to tell someone something?

Have you ever forgotten to take something
with you?

Have you ever forgotten and left something behind?

Forgetting something can frustrate you.

It can frustrate others as well.

You can avoid being forgetful.

There are things you can do to help you remember.

Get in the habit of asking yourself this question before you go from place to place:

"Am I forgetting anything?"

Ask someone to remind you about something you do not want to forget.

Write yourself a note to help you remember something.

Pin it to yourself, or put it in a place where you are sure to see it.

Write yourself a note or make a reminder mark on the back of your hand so that you won't forget something. You can use a washable ink pen to do this.

Tie a string around your finger. Make sure you do not tie it too tightly. The string will feel uncomfortable. As you become aware of it, you will remember to do what you need to do. If you do not want to use string, you can use a bandaid.

Put things in a special place so that you will not forget to take them with you. A good place is next to the door through which you'll be leaving.

Being forgetful can be frustrating.

It is important that you try not to forget things.